To:

Ted

From:

Liz

Why:

_____

_____

_____

The Way You Look Tonight

LYRICS BY DOROTHY FIELDS
INTRODUCTION BY FRANK SINATRA

RUTLEDGE HILL PRESS® • NASHVILLE, TENNESSEE
A DIVISION OF THOMAS NELSON, INC.
www.ThomasNelson.com

Front Endsheet 2 photo: Digital Vision   Front Endsheet 4 photo: Photodisc
Back Endsheet 1 photo: Digital Vision   Back Endsheets 2-3 photo: Photodisc
Photos on pages 18–19, 26–27, 32–33, 40–41, 44–45, 51, 54–55 licensed through Digital Vision.
Photos on pages 3, 8–9, 14–15, 20–21, 25, 36, 42–43, 47, 52–53, 58–59, 61 licensed through Photodisc.
Photos on pages 6, 10, 16–17, 28, 30, 38, 48–49, 56, 63 licensed through Eyewire Photos.
Photo on pages 12–13 licensed through Nova Development Corporation.

Design by OneWomanShow Design, Franklin, TN.

ISBN: 1-55853-943-3

Printed in the United States of America

01 02 03 04 05 – 5 4 3 2 1

Dearest Ted,

Despite the col___rently ___
Frank Sinatra led, he ___ woman." He was
the art of "how to tre___ woman." He was
from an era I'm afra___ we will never see the
likes of again. Not ___at you need any pointers
(you got the girl, right?), but Frank's advice
might help you keep marital bliss for the
next 50 years. I wish you much love and
hap___s. Liz

Read on····

(CD enclosed)

I think my real ambition is to pass on to others what I know. It took me a long, long time to learn these things and I don't want these lessons to die with me.

I believe in giving a woman a lot of time to make up her mind about the guy she wants to spend the rest of her life with. A man just doesn't like being crowded with female claustrophobia.

I believe the most important thing to look for in a woman is a sense of humor. Make her feel appreciated. Make her feel beautiful. If you practice long enough, you will know when you get it right.

I believe that all women should be treated like I want my wife, daughters, and granddaughters to be treated. I notice that good manners — like standing up when a woman enters the room, helping a woman on with her coat, letting her enter an elevator first, taking her arm to cross the street — are sometimes considered unnecessary or a throwback. These are habits I could never break, nor would I want to. No woman is offended by politeness.

Most of all, I believe a simple "I love you" means more than money. Tell her, "I will feel a glow just thinking of you" . . . "your smile so warm and your cheeks so soft," "that laugh that wrinkles your nose," your "breathless charm," ". . . never, ever change." "I love you . . . just the way you look tonight."

—FRANK SINATRA

The Way You Look Tonight

Some day, when I'm awfully low,
When the world is cold,
I will feel a glow just thinking of you . . .
And the way you look tonight.

Yes, you're lovely, with your smile so warm
And your cheeks so soft,
There is nothing for me but to love you,
And the way you look tonight.

With each word your tenderness grows,
Tearing my fear apart . . .
And that laugh that wrinkles your nose,
It touches my foolish heart.

Lovely . . . Never, ever change
Keep that breathless charm.
Won't you please arrange it?
'Cause I love you . . . just the way you look tonight.

Some day, when I'm

"**One word** frees us
of all the weight
and pain of life;
that word is **love.**"
—Sophocles

awfully low

"To love and be loved is to **feel the sun** from both sides."

—*David Viscott*

When
the world
is
cold,

I will feel a glow

" To me **you are** the gate of paradise. For you I renounce fame, creativity, **everything**. "
—*Frédéric Chopin*

just thinking of you. . .

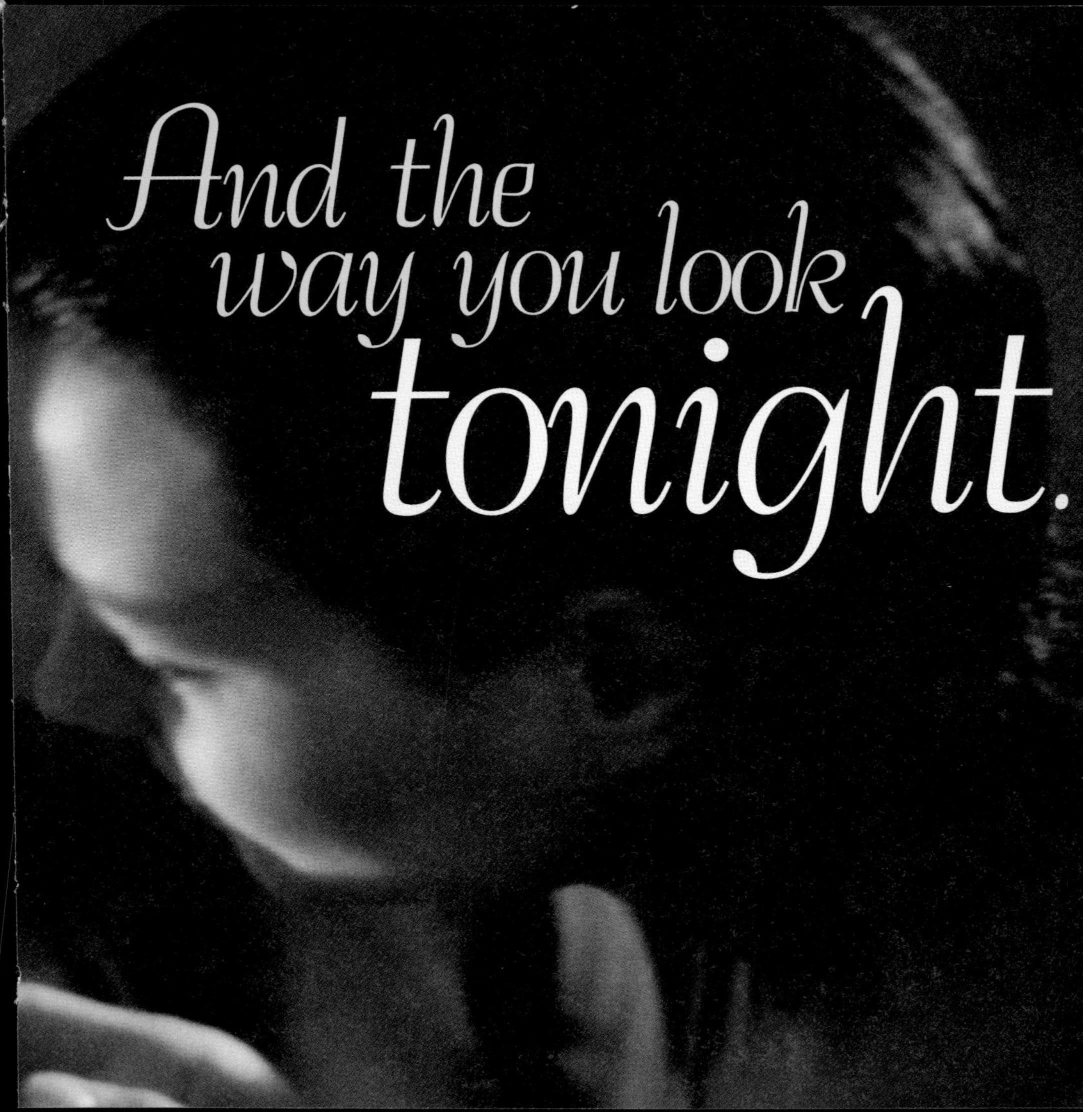
And the
way you look
tonight.

**"But to see her
was to love her,
love but her,
and love her
forever."**
—Robert Burns

you're lovely,

with your smile

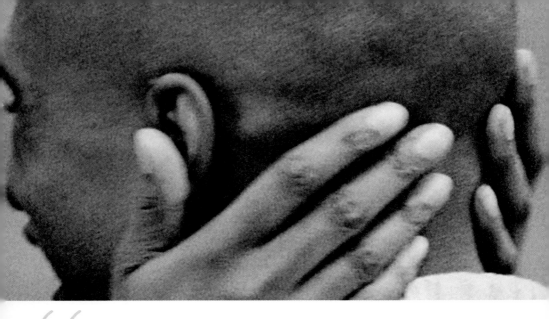

"You are always new. The last of your kisses was
ever **the sweetest**; the smile **the brightest**;
the last movement **the gracefullest**."

—*John Keats*

so warm

" " The **eyes** start love.
Intimacy perfects it. " "
—*Publilius Syrus*

And your cheeks so soft,

" Two things that
a man can't hide:
that he is drunk,
and that
*he is in
love.*"
—*Antiphanes*

There is nothing
for me but to love you,

And
the way
you look

There is only _one happiness_ in life — to love and to be loved.

—George Sand

"**Desire,**
even in its
wildest tantrums,
can neither persuade me
it is love,
nor stop me
wishing
it were."

—*W. H. Auden*

" Being with you is
like walking on a
very clear morning
— definitely
the sensation of

belonging
there."

—*E. B. White*

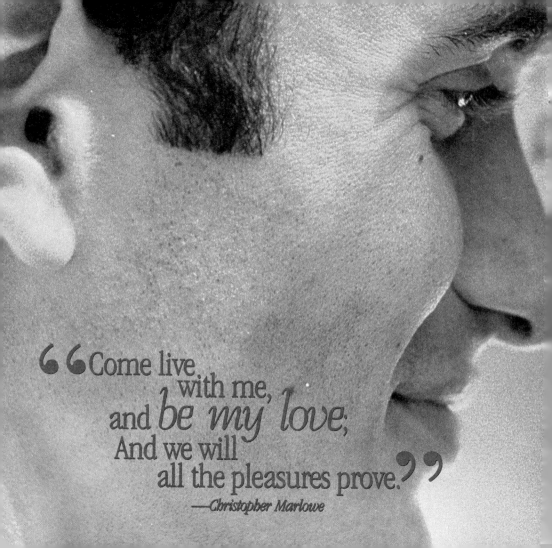

"Come live with me, and *be my love,* And we will all the pleasures prove." *—Christopher Marlowe*

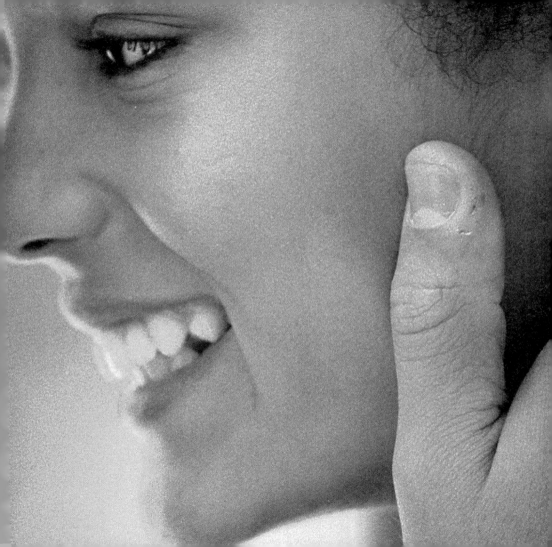

With each word your

" "Gravitation cannot be held responsible for people falling in love."
—*Albert Einstein*

tenderness grows,

" Love is the triumph of imagination **over** intelligence. **"**

—*H. L. Mencken*

Tearing my fear apart . . .

"What a grand thing,
to be loved.
What a
grander thing still,
to love."

—*Victor Hugo*

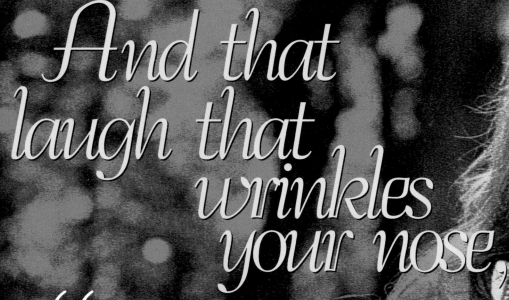

And that laugh that wrinkles your nose,

"To get the **full value of joy,** you must have someone to divide it with."

—*Mark Twain*

It touches my

foolish heart.

"To **love** someone means to see him as **God intended.**"

—*Fyodor Dostoyevsky*

*Lovely . . . .
Never, ever
change*

"If I know
what love is,
it is **because
of you**."

—*Hermann Hesse*

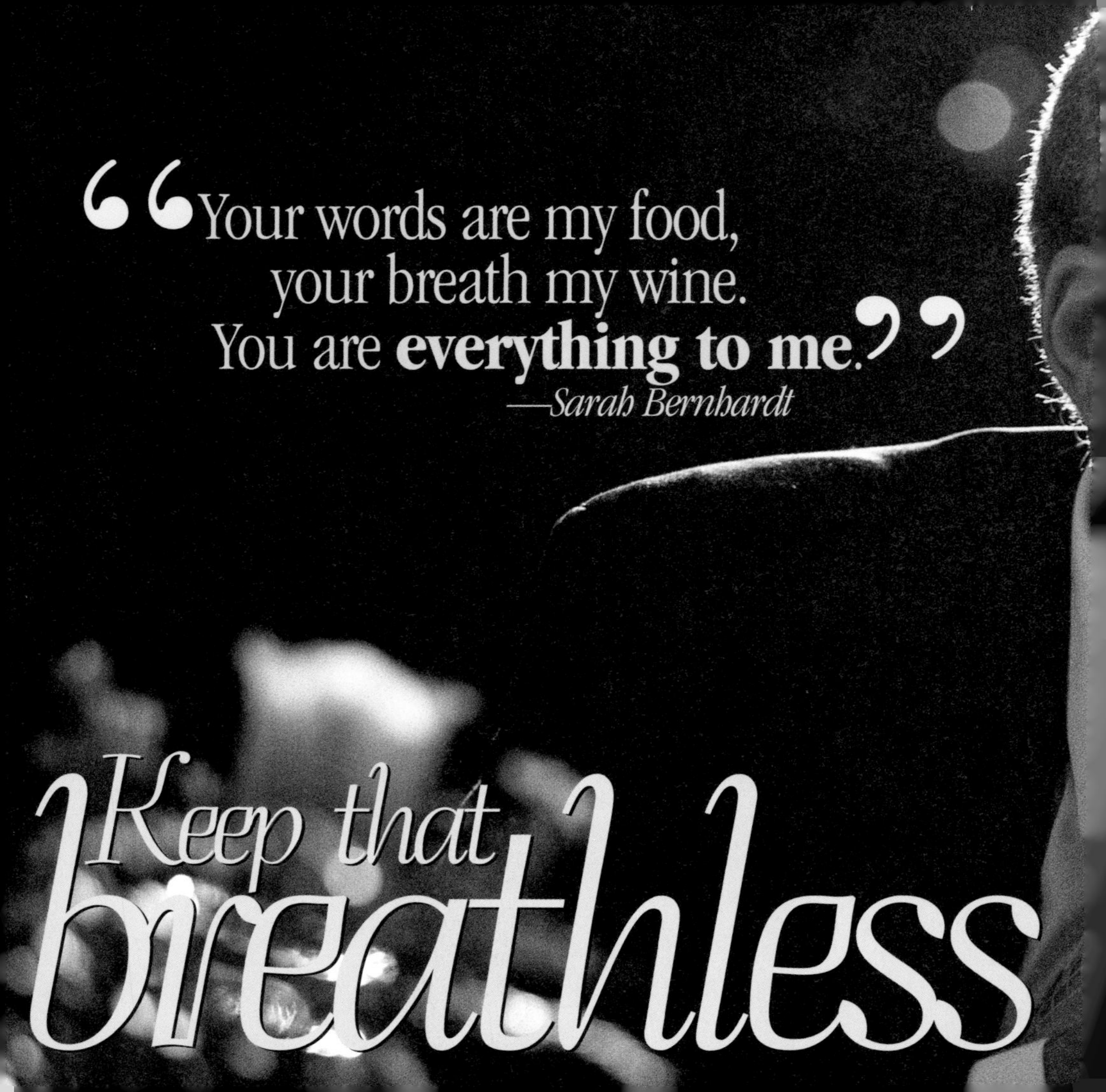
"Your words are my food,
your breath my wine.
You are **everything to me**."
—*Sarah Bernhardt*
Keep that
breathless

"Love is an *irresistible desire* to be irresistibly desired."

—*Robert Frost*

> "To love someone deeply gives you strength. Being **loved** by someone **deeply** gives you courage."
> —*Lao Tzu*

Won't

*you please
arrange it?*

"**Love** is the only flower that **grows** and **blossoms** without the aid of seasons."

—*Kahlil Gibran*

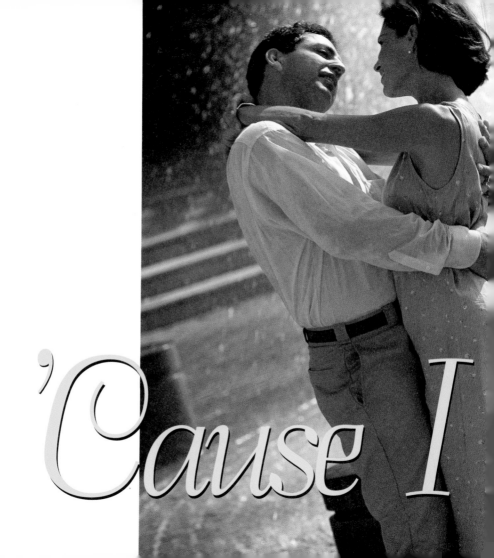

'Cause I

"Love comforteth like sunshine after rain."

—*William Shakespeare*

love you...

"When you *love someone,* all your saved up *wishes start* coming out."

—*Elizabeth Bowen*

"*A simple*
I love you
means more
than money."
—*Frank Sinatra*

*just the way
you look
tonight.*

"There is no remedy for love but to *love more.*"

—Henry Davud Thoreau